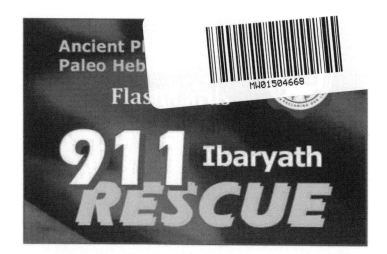

Ancient Pl...
Paleo Heb...

Flash...

911 Ibaryath
RESCUE

For Father-Son Bonding   Absolute Beginners Level

Learn **Paleo-Hebrew**
Alef-Bet

✔ Free Notebook (56 Pages)
✔ Learn The Hebrew Alef-Bet
✔ Early, Middle & Late Scripts
✔ 66 Pictographs
✔ 23 Pictures

✔ 66 Handwriting Exercises
✔ Pronunciation
Color Edition

Hebrew Israelites

Phoenician Hebrew Course
(Ancient and Paleo)

Free Live Online Ancient Phoenician Paleo Hebrew Course

Course offered monthly | 25 per class

To Enroll: zionlawschool.org/course-library

Requirement: 911 Ibaryath Rescue | Ancient Phoenician Paleo Hebrew International Edition

Ancient Phoenician Paleo Hebrew
International Edition

ZION
Law School

911 Ibaryath RESCUE

Jeremiah 8:8 How can you say, "We're wise, and the Law of The Most High is with us," when, in fact, the deceitful pen of the scribe has made it into something that deceives.

Uncover Scribal Errors & Outright Deception
Never Get Duped Again!
Authentic Pictograph Sounds

House of Yashar'al

Adults & Children
Beginners Level: Color Edition

Paleo-Ivriyt

Aleph Taw Aleph-Bet

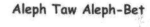

- ✔ Free Notebook (56 Pages)
- ✔ Paleo-Hebrew Aleph-Bet
- ✔ Early, Middle & Late Scripts
- ✔ 67 Pictographs
- ✔ 23 Pictures

- ✔ 67 Handwriting Exercises
- ✔ Pronunciation
- ✔ Modern Hebrew Script
  - ✔ 22 Pictographs & 22 Handwriting Exercises Pronunciation

For Mother-Daughter Bonding   Absolute Beginners Level

Learn Paleo-Hebrew
Alef-Bet

- ✔ Free Notebook (56 Pages)
- ✔ Learn The Hebrew Alef-Bet
- ✔ Early, Middle & Late Scripts
- ✔ 67 Pictographs
- ✔ 23 Pictures

- ✔ 67 Handwriting Exercises
- ✔ Pronunciation

Color Edition

Hebrew Israelites

Dr. Yasapa Yachaana, MD, MBA
Founder of Zion Law School

Phoenician Hebrew 101

A Step By Step Guide On How to Read Biblical Phoenician Hebrew

Deconstruction & Examination of Every Phoenician Hebrew Word & Sentence in the Ten Commandments

Independently published

Zion Law School
www.zionlawschool.org

Yachaana, Dr. Yasapa

I Can Read | Phoenician Hebrew

Biblical Hebrew
Ancient Phoenician Paleo Hebrew
Hebrew
Religion
Biblical Reference
Language Study
Bible

ISBN: 9798630499196

DEDICATION

This work is dedicated to the entire House of Yasharala.

ACKNOWLEDGMENTS

I want to acknowledge and say a special thank you to my dear friends and Zion Law School Scholars Derek Hawker, Hadar Jonas, Fredah Kaaria, and Jessica Finazzo for making this work possible.

CONTENTS

Deuteronomy 28:1-14 | The Blessing
1611 Authorized King James Version

AUTHOR'S NOTE

 I Can Read | Phoenician Hebrew represents the basics of phonology, morphology, and syntax (sentence structure) of the original Biblical Hebrew (Phoenician Hebrew). This work will put you firmly on the path of basic Ibaryath Literacy.

This work's major purpose is for Scholars to practice speaking and pronouncing the "Blessings" exactly as our ancient pronounced them.

The major purpose of this work is to teach you how to comfortably and confidently speak and pronounce the "Blessings" recorded at Deuteronomy 28:1-14 exactly as Moses and our ancient ancestors pronounced them. We present these verses in the Paleo Phoenician Hebrew script.

This work emphasizes reading and pronunciation skills development. It does not address the historical development of Phoenician Hebrew script nor does it present a comparative analysis of Canaanite or Schematic languages.

I use simple, easy to understand English to explain the grammar rules used to construct Phoenician

Hebrew words. A Transliteration answer key is located at the back of this work. I highly recommend writing every Phoenician Hebrew word in Deuteronomy 28:1-14 in the paleo script, and transliterate them. Practice reading, speaking and pronouncing the "Blessings" every day. This is a very effective way to develop your reading and pronunciation skills and puts you firmly on the path to Ibaryath literacy.

Visit us online at zionlawschool.org if you want to learn more about Phoenician Hebrew or our Hebraic culture and heritage. We look forward to seeing you in class!

Dr. Yasapa

Dr. Yasapa, MD, MBA
Founder of Zion Law School

FREE LIVE ONLINE COURSES

Zion Law School offers 2 Free Live Online courses. Visit us online at zionlawschool.org to enroll and reserve your seat.

1. 101 Free Live Online 8-Week Ancient Phoenician Paleo Hebrew

   a. Course textbook:

      i. <u>The 911 Ibaryath Rescue | Ancient Phoenician Paleo Hebrew</u>

      ii. This book prepares beginner Scholars to easily comprehend the <u>I Can Read | Phoenician Hebrew</u> book and to matriculate to the 101 Speaking and Reading Phoenician Hebrew course.

   b. Class size: 25

   c. Schedule: Determined by a majority vote of students on the first day of class. Once set, it will not change, so be present if you want to have a say on when your class will meet.

d. Requirements:

   i. No previous Phoenician Hebrew Language skills

   ii. Internet access, computer, laptop, cell phone with a camera and microphone

   iii. Classroom participation is mandatory

2. 101 Free Live Online 6-Week Speaking and Reading Skills

   a. Course textbook:

      i. <u>I Can Read | Phoenician Hebrew</u>

      ii. This book prepares Scholars to easily comprehend the <u>Phoenician Hebrew 101</u> book, matriculate to the 502 Ten Commandments course, and for more advanced books and courses.

   b. Class size: 25

c. Schedule: Determined by a majority vote of students on the first day of class. Once set, it will not change, so be present if you want to have a say on when your class will meet.

d. Requirements:

i. Successful completion of 101 Free Live Online 8-Week Ancient Phoenician Paleo Hebrew course

ii. Internet access, computer, laptop, cell phone with a camera and microphone

iii. Classroom participation is mandatory

PHOENICIAN HEBREW GRAMMAR

Introduction

In this section, we will introduce you to more basics of Biblical Phoenician Hebrew phonology, Morphology, and syntax. Mastery of these concepts is critically important to understanding the original Biblical Phoenician Hebrew.

Zion Law School wants to assist you in your endeavor to learn our National Language. Our teaching methodology is fun, interactive, entertaining, and thorough. Zion Law School teaches pure Phoenician Hebrew - we are the best Phoenician Hebrew school in the world. We offer a wide range of Phoenician Hebrew and English Language courses. Visit us online at zionlawschool.org to check out our courses, diploma and certificate programs, and our unique Phoenician Hebrew products and services.

Phoenician Hebrew Scripts

The starting point of your journey to reclaim your National Language and heritage is to learn the ancient, paleo and late Phoenician Hebrew pictographs and all their related information. Sight recognition of the pictographs is extremely helpful as you learn to read and look up words in a Hebrew Lexicon. As a starting point, we strongly recommend you enroll in the following courses:

1) 101 Free Live Online Ancient Phoenician Paleo Hebrew course offered by Zion Law School. You are required to order <u>911 Ibaryath Rescue | Ancient Phoenician Paleo Hebrew (International Edition)</u> to qualify to take this course.

2) 101 Free Live Online 6-Week Speaking and Reading Skills. You are required to order <u>I Can Read|Phoenician Hebrew</u> and to have completed 101 Free Live Online Ancient Phoenician Paleo Hebrew course to qualify to take this course.

3) 504 Ten Commandments Course offered by Zion Law School. You are required to order <u>Phoenician Hebrew 101</u> and to have completed 101 Speaking and Reading Phoenician Hebrew to qualify to take this course.

Zion Law School professors are bloodline ascendants of the House of Ya-Sha-Ra-La. We care about you, your family, and our Nation. Zion Law School offers the most comprehensive Ibaryatha courses in the world. In addition to learning our National Language, you will learn our ancient Hebraic culture and heritage in our classes. We look forward to guiding you on your journey to reclaim your nationality and heritage. Blessings up curses down! Riches, wealth and rulership are yours if you return to The Most High your power. Qama Yasharala!

How to Read Phoenician Hebrew

Phoenician Hebrew is read from right to left. All Phoenician Hebrew pictographs are consonants and are pronounced with consonant sounds. ("Ah" and "I" are not vowel sounds). If you want to know more about this topic, visit Zion Law School online at <u>zionlawschool.org</u> and enroll in a class.

Phoenician Hebrew Roots Word System

Root words are vowelless, unpronounceable, and represent the common foundation of the verbal and nominal stems. Stated differently, stem words are formed from their root words. For example, the root word 𐤊𐤋𐤌 (Ma-La-Ka) means "rule". As a verb stem 𐤊𐤋𐤌 means "he has reigned," "they rule" etc., and as a noun-stem 𐤊𐤋𐤌 means "king, queen, ruler" etc.

Parent Roots: The basic form of any Hebrew word is the root word. Parent roots are the most basic root and are formed from two consonants.

Child Roots: Child roots are formed from parent roots.

Words: Words are formed from child roots.

Phoenician Hebrew Pictographs			
Pictograph	**Sound**	**Vocabulary Word**	**Strong's # & Meaning**
𐤀	Ah	𐤀𐤁	Strong's #1: father, forefather, ancestor
𐤁	Ba	𐤁𐤅𐤀	Strong's #935: to enter, come or go in
𐤂	Ga	𐤂𐤀	Strong's #1341: haughty
𐤃	Da	𐤃𐤀𐤁	Strong's #1669: to pine
𐤄	Ha	𐤄𐤁𐤋	Strong's #1891: to be vain in act, word or expectation
𐤅	Wa	𐤅𐤃𐤍	Strong's #2051: a place in Arabia (Aden), to signify two rivers
𐤆	Za	𐤆𐤀𐤁	Strong's #2061: to be yellow, a wolf
𐤇	Chaa	𐤇𐤁𐤀	Strong's #2244: to secrete
𐤈	Ta	𐤈𐤀𐤁	Strong's #2868: to rejoice
𐤉	Ya	𐤉𐤀𐤁	Strong's #2968: to desire
𐤊	Ka	𐤊𐤀𐤁	Strong's #3510: to feel pain; by implication to grieve
𐤋	La	𐤋𐤁	Strong's #3820: the heart, center of anything
𐤌	Ma	𐤌𐤀𐤃	Strong's #3966: vehemence, by implication wholely, speedily, etc.
𐤍	Na	𐤍𐤀𐤄	Strong's #4999: a home
𐤎	Sa	𐤎𐤁𐤀	Strong's #5433: to quaff to satiety, i.e., become tipsy
𐤏	I	𐤏𐤁	Strong's #5645: an envelope (darkness or density), a (scud) cloud, a corpse
𐤐	Pa	𐤐𐤀𐤄	Strong's #6284: to puff, i.e. blow away
𐤑	Taza	𐤑𐤁𐤀	Strong's #6633: to mass (an army or servants)
𐤒	Qa	𐤒𐤉𐤀	Strong's #6892: vomit
𐤓	Ra	𐤓𐤀𐤄	Strong's #7200: to see
𐤔	Sha	𐤔𐤀𐤁	Strong's #7579: to bale up water
𐤕	Tha	𐤕𐤀𐤁	Strong's #8373: to desire

Verb Forms: There are seven verb forms in Phoenician Hebrew. A verb form is a combination of a root word and affixes (suffixes, prefixes, and infixes) that follow a specific configuration. Sight recognition of affixes is the master key to identifying root words. To identify the root in a word simply eliminate the affixes.

Here is an example of how your knowledge of Phoenician Hebrew prefixes can help you to easily identify the root in a *word:* The word 𐤀𐤄𐤉𐤄 is rendered "I will exist" and "I exist". To reveal its root word, we must identify and delete all prefixes and suffixes as shown here 𐤀𐤄𐤉𐤄. What remains is the root word 𐤄𐤉𐤄 which means "be" or "create"

Here is an example of how your knowledge of Phoenician Hebrew suffixes can help you to easily identify the root in a word: The word 𐤄𐤉𐤄𐤕𐤉 means "I existed" and is constructed by attaching the suffix 𐤕𐤉 + 𐤄𐤉𐤄. To reveal its root word, we must identify and delete all prefixes and suffixes attached to the word as shown here 𐤄𐤉𐤄𐤕𐤉. What remains is the root word 𐤄𐤉𐤄 which means "be" or "create".

Some words do not have a root word but are constructed from a prefix and suffix. For example, the word ⵓ⍀ (La-Ka) which means "to you" is formed from the prefix ⍀ that means "to" and the suffix ⵓ that means "you".

Prefixes

Prefixes are pictographs that are inserted in front of the first pictograph in a root word. Each prefix has its own unique meaning. Some words are formed by adding one or more prefixes to a root word. The meaning of these words is always similar to the meaning of the root word from which they are derived.

Prefixes			
And	Root word ⵝ	Like	Root word ⵓ
The	Root word ⩓	Who, which	Root word W
To	Root word ⍀	From	Root word ⵔ
In	Root word Ⳙ		

Nouns

Phoenician Hebrew nouns indicate a person (Derek, Hadar, Fredah, Jessica, Yasharala, doctor, etc.), place (school, home, etc.), thing (house, cow, etc.) or idea (love, truth, wisdom, loyalty, anger, etc.). Nouns are either masculine, feminine, or both (rare).

In Phoenician Hebrew, gender is grammatical, not natural gender (male/female) although grammatical and natural gender corresponds in the majority of Phoenician Hebrew words. Gender determines the endings a noun will take when pluralizing it. The number of a noun may be singular, plural or dual (two of the same things).

Plural Nouns

Masculine plural nouns are formed by attaching the plural suffix 𐤉𐤌 to the noun. Plural feminine nouns are made plural by attaching the feminine plural suffix 𐤕𐤀 to the feminine noun as shown in the table below.

How Make Nouns		
	Masculine Nouns Suffix	Feminine Nouns Suffix
Singular	-	𐤄 Root word
Masculine	𐤉𐤌 Root word	𐤕𐤀 Root word
Dual	𐤉𐤌 Root word	𐤉𐤌𐤕 Root word

The Ibaryatha word that means "horse" is the noun 𐤎𐤅𐤎. The Ibaryatha word that means "law" is the noun 𐤕𐤅𐤀. The table below shows how these nouns are given gender and number.

Pluralized Nouns Examples		
	Masculine Nouns Suffix	Feminine Nouns Suffix
Singular	⟨ꓩꓛꓩ⟩	⟨ꓩꓔꓡ⟩
Masculine	⟨ꓮꓔꓩꓔꓩ⟩	⟨ꓡꓔꓩꓔꓡ⟩
Dual	⟨ꓮꓔꓩꓔꓩ⟩	⟨ꓮꓔꓡꓩꓔꓡ⟩

As discussed previously, the word ⟨ꓩꓛꓩ⟩ (Ma-La-Ka) means "rule". The noun ⟨ꓩꓝꓷ⟩ (Da-Ba-Ra) means words. Observe how these nouns are pluralized in the table below.

More Pluralized Nouns				
Masculine Singular	Masculine Plural	Feminine Singular	Feminine Plural	Mas/Fem/ Dual
⟨ꓮꓛꓩ⟩	⟨ꓮꓔꓮꓛꓩ⟩	⟨ꓮꓩꓛꓩ⟩	⟨ꓡꓔꓮꓛꓩ⟩	⟨ꓮꓔꓮꓔ⟩
⟨ꓩꓝꓷ⟩	⟨ꓮꓔꓩꓝꓷ⟩	⟨ꓡꓝ⟩	⟨ꓡꓔꓩꓝ⟩	⟨ꓮꓔꓷꓔ⟩
⟨ꓷꓛꓔ⟩	⟨ꓮꓔꓷꓛꓔ⟩	⟨ꓮꓩꓔꓧ⟩	⟨ꓡꓔꓩꓔꓧ⟩	⟨ꓮꓔꓛꓔꓩ⟩

Ancient masculine nouns such as ⟨ꓩꓔꓮ⟩ (Ah-Wa-Ra), which means "light", is formed by attaching the ancient plural masculine suffix ⟨ꓡꓔ⟩ to ⟨ꓩꓔꓮ⟩ (Ah-Wa-Ra) as shown here:

⟨ꓩꓔꓮ⟩ (Ah-Wa-Ra, ancient noun) + ⟨ꓡꓔ⟩ (Wa-Tha, ancient plural suffix) forms the ancient plural noun

𐤗𐤙𐤉𐤙𐤀 (Ah-Wa-Ra-Wa-Tha) that means fathers.

Ancient plural feminine nouns are formed by attaching the ancient plural feminine suffix 𐤙𐤉 (Ya-Ma) to the ancient feminine noun.

Noun Derivatives

The table below presents the most common prefixes infixes, and suffixes inserted in noun roots to form new words called noun derivatives. All noun derivatives have similar meanings to the roots from which they are formed. This is why a good vocabulary of Ibaryatha root words is essential to Ibaryatha literacy. The minimum expectation we must demand from every bloodline ascendant of the House of Yasharala is a good working vocabulary of Ibaryatha root words.

How to Construct Noun Derivatives		
Root word𐤉	𐤉Root word	R𐤉oot word
Root word𐤀	𐤀Root word	R𐤓oot word
𐤄Root word	𐤓𐤀Root word	𐤉𐤓Root word
	𐤀𐤉Root word	

Pronouns

You need a good working vocabulary of pronouns to adequately comprehend Scriptures written in Biblical Phoenician Hebrew. You can achieve this by studying the Phoenician Hebrew Pronouns table below.

Pronouns			
Masculine			
Singular		**Plural**	
I	𐤀𐤍𐤉	We	𐤀𐤍𐤇
You	𐤀𐤕𐤄	You	𐤀𐤕𐤌
He	𐤄𐤅𐤀	They	𐤄𐤌
Feminine			
I	𐤀𐤍𐤉	We	𐤀𐤍𐤇
You	𐤀𐤕	You	𐤀𐤕𐤍
He	𐤄𐤉𐤀	They	𐤄𐤍
Possessive Pronouns			
Masculine			
Singular		**Plural**	
My	𐤉 noun	Our	𐤍𐤅 noun
Your	𐤊 noun	Your	𐤊𐤌 noun
His	𐤅 noun	Their	𐤌 noun
Feminine			
My	𐤉 noun	Our	𐤍𐤅 noun
Your	𐤊 noun	Your	𐤊𐤍 noun
Her	𐤄 noun	Their	𐤍 noun

Prepositions

Phoenician Hebrew prepositions describe spatial, temporal and other relationships between words. This section focuses on spatial (above, below, middle, besides, next to, beneath, etc.) and temporal (before, during, after, etc.) relationship. The word that occurs after a preposition is called the object of the preposition.

Prepositions		
Preposition	**Noun with Article**	**Sentence**
before	the king	Before the king
under	the tree	Under the tree
after	the flood	after the flood
between	the waters	between the waters
in, by, with	-	-
to, for	-	-
like, as, according too	-	-

Definite Direct Object Marker

In Phoenician Hebrew, direct objects are words that receive the action of verbs. ✗✗ (Ah-Tha) is an untranslatable word called the "direct object marker". Its grammatical function is to point to a definite direct object(s). ✗✗ (Ah-Tha) is spelled the same as the preposition ✗✗ (Ah-Tha) that means "with". Context is the key to determine if ✗✗ (Ah-Tha) is a direct object marker or the preposition "with".

Verbs

Verbs are words that describe actions (he runs) or states of being (he is brilliant). All bloodline ascendants of the House of Yasharal must "overstand" the form, function, and meaning of the Phoenician Hebrew verbal system to achieve a minimal level of Ibaryatha literary.

Nouns have verbal counterparts. They are spelled the same and have similar meanings because they share a common parent or child root word. Roots are 2 or 3 pictographs unpronounceable words that represent the origin of all words that stem from them. The meaning of root words is always more general than all words that originate from them.

In Phoenician Hebrew, there are 8 verbal conjugations (Perfect, imperfect, Imperative,

Cohortative, Jussive, Infinitive Construct, Infinitive Absolute, and Participle) and seven verbal forms.

If you want to learn more about the verbal root word system, order Phoenician Hebrew 101 published by Zion Law School and visit us online at zionlawschool.org to enroll in one of our classes.

Verb Tenses
"Tense" here refers to the relationship between the time of an action and the time of speaking. Completed actions are categorized as Perfect tense. Incomplete actions are categorized as Imperfect tense. Here are some examples of completed and incomplete actions:

Perfect Tense (Completed Actions)

1. Jessica hopped

2. Hadar swam

3. Derek ran

4. Fredah played

Imperfect Tense (Incomplete Actions)

1. "Jessica is hoping", "Jessica will hop"

2. "Hadar is swimming", "Hadar will swim"

3. "Derek is running", "Derek will run"

4. "Fredah is playing", "Fredah will play"

Indeed, we have not even scratched the surface of this critically important and complex topic because it is beyond the scope of this work. We would love to teach you all there is to know about Phoenician Hebrew verb tenses. Visit Zion Law School online at zionlawschool.org and enroll in a class to get started. Our teaching methodology and presentation is exciting, captivating, entertaining. We make learning fun and difficult topics easy to understand—all at an affordable price. Zion Law School is the best Phoenician Hebrew School on the planet! Be a part of something great, enroll today!

Verbs and Their Subjects
Phoenician Hebrew verbs convey the following information about their subjects:

1. Tense (perfect or imperfect)

2. Person (first, second or third person)

3. Gender (masculine or feminine)
4. Number (singular or plural)

Here is an example of the information imperfect tense verbs convey about their subjects:

Root word: ᗅ⅄ᗈ (masculine, verb) means "be"

Prefix: ᐰ is the first person, masculine, singular pronoun "I"

Word Construction: ᗅ⅄ᗈ (root word) + ᐰ (prefix, first person, masculine, singular pronoun "I") forms the word ᗅ⅄ᗈᐰ

Explanation: The prefix ᐰ tells us that the root word ᗅ⅄ᗈ is expressed in the imperfect tense and that its subject is the first person, masculine, singular pronoun "I". Thus, ᗅ⅄ᗈᐰ is rendered in English, "I exist" and "I will exist".

Here is an example of the information perfect tense verbs convey about their subjects:

Root word: ᗅ⅄ᗈ (masculine, verb) means "be"
Suffix: ⅄✕ is the first person, masculine, singular pronoun "I"

Word Construction: ᗅ⅄ᗈ (root word) + ⅄✕ (suffix) forms the word ⅄✕ᗈ⅄ᗈ

Explanation: The suffix ⅄✕ tells us that the root

word ⴰⵥⴰ is expressed in the perfect tense and that its subject is the first person, masculine, singular pronoun "I". Thus, ⵥⵅⴰⵥⴰ is rendered in English, "I existed".

Copular Verbs
These are a special kind of verbs used to join an adjective or noun complement to a subject.

Perfect Tense Verb Subjects				
Masculine				
Singular			**Plural**	
I	ⵥⵅRoot word	We	ⵏⵎRoot word	
You	ⵅRoot word	You	ⵯⵅRoot word	
He	Root word	They	ⵯRoot word	
Feminine				
I	ⵥRoot word	We	ⵏⵎRoot word	
You	ⵅRoot word	You	ⵎⵅRoot word	
He	ⴰRoot word	They	ⵯRoot word	

Imperfect Tense Verb Subjects				
Masculine				
Singular			**Plural**	
I	Root wordⴽ	We	Root wordⵎ	
You	Root wordⵅ	You	ⵯRoot wordⵅ	
He	Root wordⵥ	They	ⵯRoot wordⵥ	
Feminine				

I	Root word ⋏	We	Root word ⁊
You	ⱱRoot word ✗	You	⋑⁊Root word ✗
She	Root word ✗	They	⋑⁊Root word ✗

In English, "to be" and its various equivalents are copular verbs. Copular verbs link or join the subject of a sentence to the object of a sentence as in this illustration: "the water is clean", "Yasharala is my Nation", and "My word is my bond". Observe the presence of equivalencies to the copular verb "to be" in the illustrations above.

Here are some examples of copular verbs:

1. Be (is, am, are, was, were)

2. Appear

3. Seem

4. Look

5. Sound

6. Smell

7. Taste

8. Feel

9. Become

10. Get

Copular verbs tell us that that the subject and its complement indicate or symbolize the same thing. They also tell us that the subject has the same property indicated or symbolized by its complement. *Copular verbs never show action.* Here are some examples of copular verbs:

I **am** me. (The word 'am' joins or links the subject "I" with the word "me").

That was my cat itself. (The word 'was' joins or links the subject "that" with "cat itself").

It **appears** material. (The word 'appears' joins or links the subject "It" with the word "material").

Auxiliaries Verbs
These are a tiny class of verbs that express tense, aspect, modality, and other grammatically important information. Auxiliary verbs have the following special characteristics:

1. They have contracted forms

2. They make interrogatives

3. They can be made negative by adding 'not' only

4. They are used for question phrases

5. They form different tenses

6. They are used for short answers

7. They are used for additions to remarks

8. They make the emphatic form

9. They take adverbs like always sometimes, often nearly, etc. after them

10. They have defective verbs

Here are some examples of auxiliary verbs:

1. Be (am, is, are, was, were)

2. Have (has, had)

3. Can (could)

4. Shall (should)

5. Will (would)

6. May (might)

7. Must

8. Ought

9. Do (does, did)

10. Need

11. Dare

12. Used to

Adjectives

Adjectives are words that modify, describe, characterize or classify nouns. (Only one of the above requirements must be met). Thus, adjectives increase nouns specificity, so whatever you want to say about nouns will be said with adjectives. Here are some examples of adjectives:

Noun: Car

1. A brown car
2. A big car

3. An expensive car

Noun: King

4. Strong king

5. Weak king

6. An evil king

Noun: Water

7. The blue water

8. Shallow water

9. Clean water

Noun: Food

10. The delicious food

11. Hot food

12. Spicy food

Phoenician Hebrew is written and read from right to left. Nouns are written before their adjectives. Here is an example of an adjective from Deuteronomy 28:9:

ᎳᏔᏍᏇ   ᎤᎣᏓ
Holy   as a people
Adjective noun

The word "people" is a noun. "People" is written before the word "holy", which is an adjective. The word "holy" describes, classifies, and characterizes the word "people", therefore, "holy" is an adjective.

Nouns and adjectives must agree in definiteness. Thus, if a noun has the definite article Ꭵ (the) in the prefix position, the adjective that describes that noun must also have the definite article Ꭵ (the) in the prefix position. Here is an example of definiteness of noun and adjective agreement:

ᎳᏔᏍᏇᎥ   ᎤᎣᎵᎥ
holy   as a people
adjective   noun
singular   singular

An adjective must also agree in gender and number with its noun. In the example above, ᎳᏔᏍᏇᎥ and ᎤᎣᎵᎥ are both masculine and singular in number.

How to Make Adjectives		
	Masculine Suffix	Feminine Suffix

Singular	-	𐤄
Plural	𐤉𐤌	𐤅𐤕

Now let's use this table to demonstrate how adjectives are made. The Ibaryatha word for *good* is 𐤈𐤅𐤁. The table below presents 𐤈𐤅𐤁 (good) in its various adjectival forms.

The gender of an adjective does not change the meaning of the adjective. The number of an adjective does not change the meaning of the adjective unless it is used substantively. Plural form adjectives are translated in English in the singular.

How to Pluralize Adjectives 𐤈𐤅𐤁 (Good)		
	Masculine Suffix	Feminine Suffix
Singular	𐤈𐤅𐤁 (good)	𐤈𐤅𐤁𐤄 (good)
Plural	𐤈𐤅𐤁𐤉𐤌 (goods)	𐤈𐤅𐤁𐤅𐤕 (goods)

*The masculine singular form is unchanged.

Attributive Adjectives

Attributive adjectives modify nouns. For example, the word "clean" in "the clean water" and the word "good" in "the good king" are used attributively

because they modify the nouns "water" and "king".
Here are some examples of Ibaryatha attributive
adjectives:

ⵏⵉⵊⵔⵐ ⵏⵉⵯⵯⵊⴲ: Good men
good   men

ⵏⵉⵊⵔⵐⵣ ⵏⵉⵯⵯⵊⴲⵣ: The good men
good   the men

Predicative Adjectives
These adjectives create a predicate relationship
because they assert something about nouns. They
do not modify the nouns. In the examples, the
"blessings are tangible" and "the instructions are
easy", the adjectives assert something about the
nouns, which creates a predication. Forms of the
verb "to be" create a predication or predicate
relationship in English.

In Ibaryatha, a predication or predicate relationship
is created when an adjective agrees with its noun in
gender and number but not definiteness. The
predicate adjective never takes the definite article ⵣ
(the) and may come before or after its noun. Here is
an example of a predication:

ⵊⵔⵐ ⵯⵉⵯⵣ: The man is good
good the man

𐤅𐤋𐤀𐤄 𐤋𐤊𐤈: The man is good
the man good

In the above usage, there is no Phoenician Hebrew verb form of "to be" in either sentence. Due to the presence of the predicate relationship demonstrated by the lack of agreement (mismatch) of definiteness, both sentences are translated with the word "is" between the noun and the adjective. Whenever nouns and adjectives do not agree in definiteness, it indicates a predicative relationship between the nouns and adjectives.

Substantive Adjectives
These adjectives are used independently as nouns. In other words, there are no nouns for these adjectives to modify. Here is an example of a substantive adjective:

𐤇𐤊𐤌 is an adjective that means "wise". 𐤇𐤊𐤌 (wise) used substantively, by itself, it is translated in English as "a wise one" or "a wise man". When the definite article is present as shown here, 𐤄𐤇𐤊𐤌, is translated in English as "the wise one" or "the wise man".

Interrogatives
Interrogative sentences are those sentences whose **grammatical** form reveals that they are questions. An interrogative sentence is shown

whenever any one of the pictographs listed below is prefixed to the first word of a Phoenician Hebrew sentence. When 𐤄 is prefixed to the first word of a sentence it is called "Interrogative 𐤄" and the sentence is, therefore, an interrogative sentence. For example, 𐤏𐤕𐤃𐤅𐤏 means "you know" in English, however, its meaning changes to "do you know?" when "Interrogative 𐤄" is prefixed to it as shown here, 𐤄𐤏𐤃𐤅𐤏.

Words that make a sentence an interrogative sentence:

𐤅𐤌   Who

𐤄𐤌   What

𐤅𐤕𐤌   When

𐤅𐤀 / 𐤄𐤍𐤅𐤀   Where

𐤋𐤌𐤄   Why

𐤉𐤅𐤀   How

READING AND PRONUNCIATION

Deuteronomy 28:1-14

[Text in Paleo-Hebrew script, verses 1–9]

Transliteration Exercises

Learning to read Phoenician Hebrew and to speak
Ibaryatha, our National Language, you must
develop sight recognition of each pictograph. You
must also memorize each pictograph's sound and
how to pronounce them. Developing the above
skills will greatly increase your joy and speed at
which you learn Phoenician Hebrew. These skills
will also make it easier for you to understand more
advanced Phoenician Hebrew books with minimal
effort on your part. Now, let's get into the
exercises!

Exercise #1

Transliterate each Phoenician Hebrew word on the
lines below:

Deuteronomy 28:1

ץץבלﬡ ﬡﬡﬡﬤ לﬡﬤﬨ ﬡﬤ﬩ﬠﬢ ﬡﬤ﬩ﬠﬧﬤ ﬨ﬩ ﬡ﬩ﬡ[1]

_____

ﬨ﬩ﬠ ﬤ﬩ﬡﬡ ﬤﬠﬡ ﬡ﬩﬩ﬡﬡ﬩ﬤ ﬠ ﬨﬡ ﬡ﬩﬩ﬡﬠ

_____

ﬤ﬩﬩ﬢ ﬤ﬩﬩ﬤ ﬠﬠ ﬡ﬩﬩ﬠﬠ ﬤﬤﬡﬠﬡ ﬡ﬩ﬡﬤ ﬤﬡﬨﬡ﬩

_____

ﬠﬨ﬩ﬡﬡ ﬤﬤﬤﬡ ﬠ﬩

_____

Exercise #2

Write each word in Deuteronomy 28:2 in the Phoenician Hebrew script. Leave space below each line to transliterate each Phoenician Hebrew word.

Deuteronomy 28:2

_____

_____

_____

_____

_____

_____

_____

Exercise #3

Write each word in Deuteronomy 28:3 in the Phoenician Hebrew script. Leave space below each line to transliterate each Phoenician Hebrew word.

Deuteronomy 28:3

_____

_____

_____

_____

_____

_____

_____

Exercise #4

Write each word in Deuteronomy 28:4 in the Phoenician Hebrew script. Leave space below each line to transliterate each Phoenician Hebrew word.

Deuteronomy 28:4

_____

_____

_____

_____

_____

_____

_____

_____

Exercise #5

Write each word in Deuteronomy 28:5 in the Phoenician Hebrew script. Leave space below each line to transliterate each Phoenician Hebrew word.

Deuteronomy 28:5

_____

_____

_____

_____

_____

_____

_____

_____

Exercise #6

Write each word in Deuteronomy 28:6 in the Phoenician Hebrew script. Leave space below each line to transliterate each Phoenician Hebrew word.

Deuteronomy 28:6

_____
_____
_____
_____
_____
_____
_____
_____

Exercise #7

Write each word in Deuteronomy 28:7 in the Phoenician Hebrew script. Leave space below each line to transliterate each Phoenician Hebrew word.

Deuteronomy 28:7

_____
_____
_____
_____
_____
_____
_____
_____

Exercise #8

Write each word in Deuteronomy 28:8 in the Phoenician Hebrew script. Leave space below each line to transliterate each Phoenician Hebrew word.

Deuteronomy 28:8

_____

_____

_____

_____

_____

_____

_____

_____

Exercise #9

Write each word in Deuteronomy 28:9 in the Phoenician Hebrew script. Leave space below each line to transliterate each Phoenician Hebrew word.

Deuteronomy 28:9

_____

_____

_____

_____

_____

_____

_____

_____

Exercise #10

Write each word in Deuteronomy 28:10 in the
Phoenician Hebrew script. Leave space below each
line to transliterate each Phoenician Hebrew word.

Deuteronomy 28:10

_____

_____

_____

_____

_____

_____

_____

Exercise #11

Write each word in Deuteronomy 28:11 in the
Phoenician Hebrew script. Leave space below each
line to transliterate each Phoenician Hebrew word.

Deuteronomy 28:11

_____

_____

_____

_____

_____

_____

_____

Exercise #12

Write each word in Deuteronomy 28:12 in the Phoenician Hebrew script. Leave space below each line to transliterate each Phoenician Hebrew word.

Deuteronomy 28:12

_____

_____

_____

_____

_____

_____

_____

Exercise #13

Write each word in Deuteronomy 28:13 in the Phoenician Hebrew script. Leave space below each line to transliterate each Phoenician Hebrew word.

Deuteronomy 28:13

_____

_____

_____

_____

_____

_____

_____

Exercise #14

Write each word in Deuteronomy 28:14 in the Phoenician Hebrew script. Leave space below each line to transliterate each Phoenician Hebrew word.

Deuteronomy 28:14

_____

_____

_____

_____

_____

_____

_____

30 Day Challenge

Your assignment for the next 30 days is to read aloud the blessings that The Most High promised us in Deuteronomy Chapter 28:1-14. Read them when you wake up and before you go to bed. Practice speaking and pronouncing each word correctly. Write them down on paper once daily for the next 30 days. Commit the "Blessings" to memory. Teach your family and friends how to speak and pronounce them correctly. You can do it! Rise, Yasharala, rise!

TRANSLITERATION ANWER KEY

Deuteronomy 28:1-14

1 WaHaYaHa AhMa ShaMaWaI ThaShaMaI

BaQaWaLa YaHaWaHa AhLaHaYaKa LaShaMaRa

LaIShaWaTha AhTha KaLa MaTazaWaThaYaWa

AhShaRa AhNaKaYa MaTazaWaKa HaYaWaMa

WaNaThaNaKa   YaHaWaHa   AhLaHaYaKa

ILaYaWaNa ILa KaLa GaWaYaYa HaAhRaTaza:

2 WaBaAhWa ILaYaKa KaLa HaBaRaKaWaTha

HaAhLaHa WaHaShaYaGaKa KaYa ThaShaMaI

BaQaWaLa YaHaWaHa AhLaHaYaKa:

3 BaRaWaKa AhThaHa BaIYaRa WaBaRaWaKa

AhThaHa BaShaDaHa:

4 BaRaWaKa PaRaYa BaTaNaKa WaPaRaYa

AhDaMaThaKa   WaPaRaYa   BaHaMaThaKa

ShaGaRa   AhLaPaYaKa   WaIShaThaRaWaTha
TazaAhNaKa:

5 BaRaWaKa TaNaAhKa WaMaShaAhRaThaKa:

6 BaRaWaKa AhThaHa BaBaAhKa WaBaRaWaKa
AhThaHa BaTazaAhThaKa:

7 YaThaNa YaHaWaHa AhTha AhYaBaYaKa

HaQaMaYaMa   ILaYaKa   NaGaPaYaMa

LaPaNaYaKa   BaDaRaKa   AhChaaDa

YaTazaAhWa   AhLaYaKa   WaBaShaBaIHa

DaRaKaYaMa YaNaWaSaWa LaPaNaYaKa:

8   YaTazaWa   YaHaWaHa   AhThaKa   AhTha

HaBaRaKaHa   BaAhSaMaYaKa   WaBaKaLa

MaShaLaChaa   YaDaChaa   WaBaRAKaLa

BaAhRaTaza AhShaRa YaHaWaHa AhLaHaYaKa

NaThaNa:

9   YaQaYaMaKa   YaHaWaHa   LaWa   LaIWa
QaDaWaSha KaAhShaRa NaShaBaI LaKa KaYa
ThaShaMaRa AhTha MaTazaWaTha YaHaWaHa
AhLaHaYaKa WaHaLaKaTha BaDaRaKaYaWa:
10 WaRaAhWa KaLa IMaYa HaAhRaTaza KaYa
ShaMa   YaHaWaHa   NaQaRaAh   ILaYaKa
WaYaRaAhWa MaMaKa:
11 WaHaWaThaRaKa YaHaWaHa LaTaWaBaHa
BaPaRaYa   BaTaNaKa   WaBaPaRaYa
BaHaMaThaKa WaBaPaRaYa AhDaMaThaKa ILa
HaAhDaMaHa AhShaRa NaShaBaI YaHaWaHa
LaAhBaThaYaKa LaThaTha LaKa:
12 YaPaThaChaa   YaHaWaHa   LaKa   AhTha
AhWaTazaRaWa   HaTaWaBa   AhTha
HaShaMaYaMa LaThaTha MaTaRa AhRaTazaKa

BaIThaWa WaLaBaRaKa AhTha KaLa MaIShaHa

YaDaKa　　　WaHaLaWaYaTha　　　GaWaYaMa

RaBaYaMa WaAhThaHa LaAh ThaLaWaHa:

13　WaNaThaNaKa　YaHaWaHa　LaRaAhSha

WaLaAh　LaZaNaBa　WaHaYaYaTha　RaQa

LaMaILaHa　WaLaAh　ThaHaYaHa　LaMaTaHa

KaYa　ThaShaMaI　AhLa　MaTazaWaTha

YaHaWaHa AhLaHaYaKa AhShaRa AhNaKaYa

MaTazaWaKa　　　HaYaWaMa　　　LaShaMaRa

WaLaIShaWaTha:

14　　　WaLaNa　　　ThaSaWaRa　　　MaKaLa

HaDaBaRaYaMa　　　AhShaRa　　　AhNaKaYa

MaTazaWaHa　　　AhThaKaMa　　　HaYaWaMa

YaMaYaNa　WaShaMaAhWaLa　LaLaKaTha

AhChaaRaYa　AhLaHaYaMa　AhChaaRaYaMa

LaIBaDaMa:

___

ABOUT THE AUTHOR

Dr. Yasapa MD, MBA

Dr. Yasapa's major purpose is to help the House of Yasharala return to the Most High. Dr. Yasapa is best known for his Free Live Online 8 Week Ancient Phoenician Paleo Hebrew Course. Dr. Yasapa is the founder of Zion Law School (zionlawschool.org) whose mission is to secure the blessing promised to the House of Yasharala in Deuteronomy Chapter 28. Dr. Yasapa is the author of 911 Ibaryath Rescue | Ancient Phoenician Paleo Hebrew, Phoenician Hebrew 101 and other Phoenician Hebrew and mixed Hebrew Language literature.

Made in the USA
Middletown, DE
28 March 2025

73391535R00035